Alfie Alligator
Isn't it Time?

Judy Hindley
Pictures by
Colin King

Collins

First published 1986 by William Collins Sons & Co Ltd, London and Glasgow
© text and illustrations Small World 1986.

Tick-tock,

Tick-tock,

Tick-tock,

BLEEEP!

Wake up, wake up!
It's seven o'clock in the morning!
Isn't it time you were up and about?
Quick, wake up!
Get up!
Get out!
Look at the sky! Look at the sun!
Look at us and Dad and Mum!
It's time to wake up at our house!

Eight o'clock, eight o'clock,
Isn't it time to go?
Around the house,
Around the block,
Everyone knows it's eight o'clock!
They're washing and dressing
And eating their toast,
And cleaning their shoes
And collecting their post,
It's time to be ready to go!

Nine o'clock, nine o'clock,
Isn't it time for school?
Hang up your coat!
Sit in your chair!
You know we can't start
Until everyone's here,
And it's time for the buzzer to go.
BUZZ!
It's time for our school to start!

BUZZ BUZZ

Ten o'clock, ten o'clock,
Isn't it time for milk?
Look at your hands!
Look at your face!
Wash out your brushes!
Clean up the place!
We're thirsty –
It's time for some milk!

Eleven o'clock, eleven o'clock,
Isn't it time to go out?
Isn't it time to sing and shout,
And jump and fight and rush about?
Everyone else wants to play.
Hey!
It's time to go out and play!

Twelve o'clock, twelve o'clock,
Isn't it time for a rest?
Isn't it time to sit quietly down,
With your feet on the floor,
And your chair on the floor,
And your head on your hands
On your desk?
Sshhh!
It's time for the story to start!

15

One o'clock, one o'clock,
Aren't you a little bit hungry yet?
There's salad and sandwiches,
Jelly and stew,
And soon there'll be nothing at all for you.
Hurry!
It's time to eat!

Two o'clock, two o'clock,
Isn't it time for a walk?
Outside in the sun,
There's a world going on,
Creeping and hopping
And flying and hiding,
Down in the puddles,
Up in the trees,
And under the stones on the lawn –
Come on!
It's time for our nature walk!

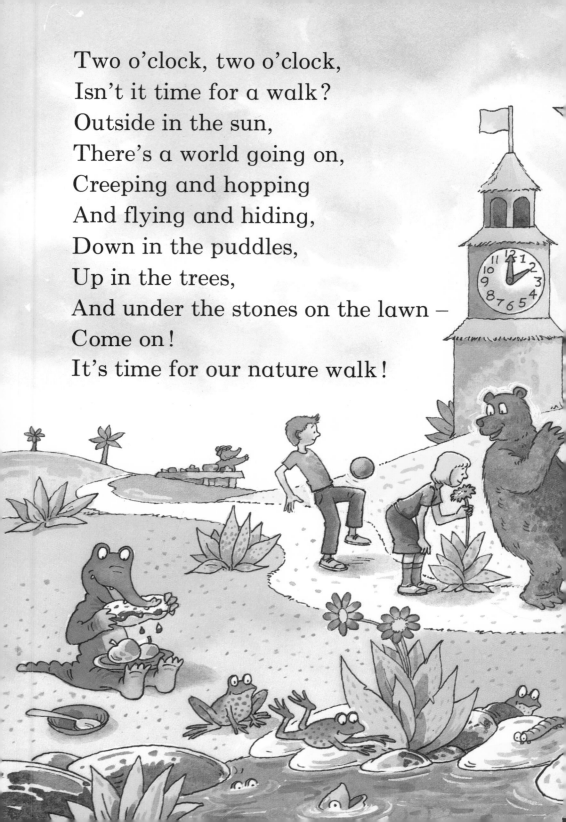

What's the time? Look at the clock –
Three o'clock!
RUN!
Time to go home
And sweep and scrub.

What a long day it's been. . . .

We had to get up at
Seven o'clock,

And be ready to go at
Eight o'clock,

And start our lessons at
Nine o'clock,

And have our milk at
Ten o'clock,

And go out to play at
Eleven o'clock,

And have our story at
Twelve o'clock,

And have something to eat at
One o'clock,

And go for our walk at
Two o'clock,

And get very busy at
Three o'clock,

Because . . .
Because at four o'clock . . .
Knock, knock, knock, knock –

IT'S TIME
FOR THE PARTY TO START!

Five o'clock, five o'clock,
Isn't it time for the games to stop?
Isn't it time for the prizes now?
Isn't it time for the sweets?
Isn't it time for the birthday cake?
Isn't it time to eat?

Six o'clock, six o'clock,
Isn't it time for the presents?
Now!
Open them up –
What's in the box?
Tick-tock –
WOW!

So isn't it time to tell the time?
Look at it –
What does it say?
Seven o'clock, seven o'clock,
The end of a wonderful day.

Sleep well, sleep tight,
It's seven o'clock, seven o'clock,
It's seven o'clock at night.

Tick-tock,
Tick-tock,
Tick-tick-tick-tick-tick. . . .